Dialogues with Silence

Prayers & Drawings

———•◆•———

THOMAS MERTON

Edited by JONATHAN MONTALDO

HarperSanFrancisco
A Division of HarperCollins*Publishers*

HarperCollins books may be purchased for educational, business, or sales promotional use. For information please write: Special Markets Department, HarperCollins Publishers, Inc., 10 East 53rd Street, New York, NY 10022.

HarperCollins Web site: http://www.harpercollins.com
HarperCollins®, ✦®, and HarperSanFrancisco™ are trademarks of HarperCollins Publishers, Inc.

FIRST HARPERCOLLINS PAPERBACK EDITION PUBLISHED IN 2004
Designed by Joseph Rutt

Library of Congress Cataloging-in-Publication Data
Merton, Thomas, 1915–1968.
Dialogues with silence : prayers & drawings/ Thomas Merton;
edited by Jonathan Montaldo.— 1st ed.
p. cm.
Includes bibliographical references.
ISBN 0–06–065603–4 (paperback)
1. Prayers. 2. Catholic Church—Prayer-books and devotions—English.
I. Montaldo, Jonathan. II. Title.
BV210.2 .M46 2001
242'.802—dc21
2001024697
04 05 06 07 08 ✦/RRD(H) 10 9 8 7 6 5 4 3 2

Dialogues with Silence
is dedicated to
Ruth Calvert Jenkins Merton
(1887–1921)
Thomas Merton's mother
whom he lost to death when he was six

You formed my inmost being.
You knitted me together in my mother's womb. . . .
You know me through and through,

My being was no mystery to you
When I was formed in secret,
Woven in the depths of the earth.
Psalm 139

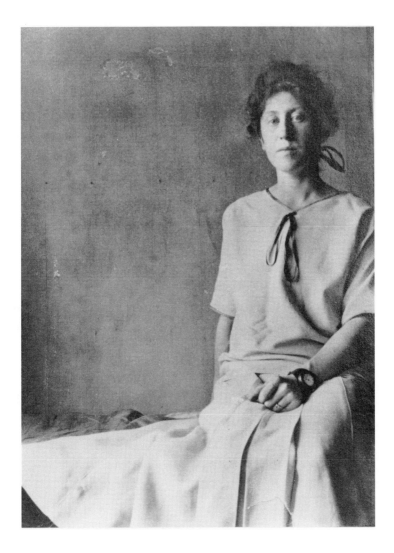

My Lord God, I have no idea where I am going.
I do not see the road ahead of me. I cannot know for certain
where it will end. Nor do I really know myself, and the fact that
I think I am following Your will does not mean that I am
actually doing so. But I believe that the desire to please You
does in fact please You. And I hope I have that desire in all that
I am doing. I hope that I will never do anything apart from that
desire. And I know that, if I do this, You will lead me by the
right road, though I may know nothing about it. Therefore I
will trust You always though I may seem to be lost and in the
shadow of death. I will not fear, for You are ever with me, and
You will never leave me to face my perils alone.

Thoughts in Solitude

Thomas Merton's
Dialogues with Silence

"The only unhappiness," Thomas Merton wrote, "is not to love God." If this standard for his joy is accurate, if what he wrote in his private journal is true, then the book you hold in your hands bears the signature in prayers and drawings of a deeply happy human being.

In defining monks, Saint Benedict, the father of Western monasticism, wrote simply that they "truly seek God." By this criterion, Thomas Merton was probably formed a monk in his mother's womb.

He was born of artists—a New Zealander and an American who found each other in a painter's studio in Paris. Retreating from the First World War and finding sanctuary in Prades, France, Owen sired, Ruth Jenkins bore, and both nourished a son who would become in time a world-celebrated monk and writer.

He came into the world, like everyone else, captive to a tainted ancestry of human selfishness, greed, and violence that would inexorably graft itself unto his own heart. By a committed life of prayer and work he would learn the right means to root out the thicket of Western culture's materialism lodged within him. He would rediscover for himself and for others reading over his shoulder a traditional road toward selflessness, generosity, and nonviolence. By his vocation to become a monk and writer, Merton would become another witness for his generation of the way out of self-defeating individualism by tracking anew the boundaries of that ancient other country whose citizens recognize a hidden ground of unity and love among all living beings.

Merton possessed a critical mind and a poet's passion. He wantonly loved books, women, ideas, art, jazz, hard drink, cigarettes, argument, and having his opinions heard. He nevertheless chose at the age of twenty-three to be baptized a Roman Catholic; then, going further at the age of twenty-six, he chose to become—to the consternation of his friends—a Trappist monk.

He had exhibited compulsions that should have made him a literary precursor to the "beat generation." Merton should have evolved into a wild man always high on a drug of choice, perpetually on the road, and writing in rebellion against the society of squares and gray suits. He enclosed himself instead in a forest monastery in the middle of America. Once a happy denizen of Manhattan, he placed himself in a subsistence farming community marked by frugal stability and routine, by a life of prayer, silence, and anonymity from the world's one thousand and one interesting things. By becoming a monk, Merton ensured that his rebellion against the world and the madness it had induced in him would go deeper than any literary pose.

On December 10, 1941, under a canopy of cold stars, Merton arrived in rural Kentucky at the Abbey of Gethsemani and immediately loved its walls. When the gatehouse door shut behind him, he abandoned his disordered youth and wedged himself into narrow borders so as to find out who he might more authentically become before he died.

Once taking up his inner journey at Gethsemani, he would never waiver for long from its hard path. He participated by writing in the political, ideological, and social storms attending three decades from the 1940s to the 1960s. He traveled through these and his own personal storms clinging until the very end to the solid mast of an ancient monastic path.

Merton's stability at Gethsemani for twenty-seven years was hard therapy for the wanderlust he had inherited from his father. Yet his monastic stability would become the great blessing for his writing, his teaching and his art. Staying in one place, he was able to delve ever more deeply by reflection and prayer into the meaning of his unfolding life in the unfolding history of his times. Merton's stability honed his art of confession and witness in poetry, journals, letters, and books on a wide range of interests. By intimately exploring a monk's spare geography, Merton discovered the riches awaiting the tireless cartographer of its limitations.

He passed over to the true geography of his heart not by crossing seas and seeking out new cities but by sinking roots in one Kentucky place with a community of fellow travelers. Rooting his mind at Gethsemani, he paradoxically experienced the wider horizons of his times. Merton's stability at Gethsemani, through the thick and the thin of his passionate struggle for a better way to be a human being, is a major key to his appeal to a generation that risked, as he himself had risked, traveling down a road of rootless dissipation.

Thomas Merton remained a monk for twenty-seven years because he could never stop loving becoming a monk. In spite of decades of monastic routine (or indeed precisely because of it), he could muster a poet's concentrated joy for the smallest turns

of difference in time or temperature that marked a day as singu-
lar and new. Merton's joy—often muffled below the voicing of
his public cares and concerns—situated him among those rare
human beings who love the life they are leading and who have
found their own true place. He reflects his typical joy as a monk
in this journal entry dated May 21, 1963:

*Marvelous vision of the hills at 7:45 A.M. The same hills as
always, as in the afternoon, but now catching the light in a
totally new way, at once very earthly and very ethereal, with del-
icate cups of shadow and dark ripples and crinkles where I had
never seen them before, the whole slightly veiled in mist so that it
seemed to be a tropical shore, a newly discovered continent. A
voice in me seemed to be crying, "Look! Look!" For these are the
discoveries, and it is for this that I am high on the mast of my
ship (have always been) and I know that we are on the right
course, for all around is the sea of paradise.*

Monastic life inculcated in Merton this heightened awareness,
an alertness to the possibilities of the hour, what he called "the grip
of the present." Alert expectancy was a habit he cultivated for a
fruitful, examined life. His monastic stability and its enclosed hori-
zons ironically made all the keener his innate tendency to be more
ready to depart than to settle down in fixed ideas or perspectives.
Merton was never afraid to walk away from himself when, through
experience, prayer, and study, he found himself still too narrow and
noninclusive to be a thoroughly catholic human being.

By appropriating the insights of a long monastic tradition,

Merton learned that waiting for a "word" he could not speak to himself was the essence of prayer. Stillness, poverty of spirit, keeping vigil, guarding thoughts, and fasting from one's own selfishness were essential attributes of his practice of monastic humanism. In one of the last books that he prepared for publication, *The Climate of Monastic Prayer*, he defined contemplation as "essentially a listening in silence" and "an expectancy":

> *The true contemplative is not one who prepares his mind for a particular message that he wants or expects to hear, but is one who remains empty because he knows that he can never expect to anticipate the words that will transform his darkness into light. He does not even anticipate a special kind of transformation. He does not demand light instead of darkness. He waits on the Word of God in silence, and, when he is "answered," it is not so much by a word that bursts into his silence. It is by his silence itself, suddenly, inexplicably revealing itself to him as a word of great power, full of the voice of God.*

His envisioning the practice of prayer as keeping one's mind awake in the dark was the mature fruit of what had already been seeded in him while still a young man. He was not at Gethsemani two weeks in 1941 before he wrote this prayer before Midnight Mass at Christmas:

> *Your brightness is my darkness. I know nothing of You and, by myself, I cannot even imagine how to go about knowing You. If I imagine You, I am mistaken. If I understand You, I am*

deluded. If I am conscious and certain I know You, I am crazy. The darkness is enough.

Merton had learned early to keep vigil in silence with his heart's eye on the horizon of the next moment. The next moment could reveal in light or in shadow the presence of the Beloved he awaited. He kept his mind's eye open for the unexpected epiphany. Waiting without projecting his own needs into the next moment became a dark form of hope. In committing some of his personal prayers to writing, Merton's gift to his readers was his honesty in communicating the darkness that was his rite of passage into God's presence.

"My Lord God, I have no idea where I am going" is the declaration that begins Merton's most famous prayer, now printed on cards that find their way to desktops, refrigerator doors, and mirrors. His acknowledged ignorance in this prayer resonates with anyone who reads it. Originally published in *Thoughts in Solitude*, his declaration of always moving forward in darkness but with hope takes its rightful place at the mast of this book. Acknowledged ignorance and hopeful insecurity were the attendant angels to Merton's monastic life and art.

Not to know where his life was going was always to begin again in Merton's journey to love learning and desire God. Ignorance acknowledged was a stimulus to new experience. Ignorance acknowledged was an exciting wisdom that poised Merton for God's "next thing."

Darkness acknowledged kept Merton leaning toward the "thin places" between night and the edge of light that signals dawn. Darkness acknowledged kept him sober and watchful, although never perfectly, so that he might not miss a gate to the rose garden or pass a door that might lead to paradise and deliverance from the cycle of loss and recovery and loss again.

Thomas Merton's literary voice has a different inflection for each of his readers. Each auditor hears a different Merton. Although he consciously invited identification with his voice, who Merton really was in all his complexity must ultimately remain a mystery. His readers have only markings, the tracks of his mind and heart—perhaps only rarely of his soul—left behind on a page. Even in his most private journals and most personal letters, his writing about himself can produce misleading photographs. A still life of a wild bird in flight, no matter how beautiful and true to the color of the creature's wings, does not reveal how the bird actually flew. A photograph catches only one frame, not the full trajectory of the flight itself.

The prayers and drawings of this book are artifacts of Merton's dialogues with silence. Placed together in this book, they resonate to reveal his desire *to return to the Father, to the Immense, to the Primordial, to the Unknown, to Him Who loves, to the Silent, to the Holy, to the Merciful, to Him Who is All.*

These prayers and drawings are relics of Merton's contemplation, not his life of contemplation itself. Placed side by side, they can virtually draw us into the real presence of that silence, that expectancy, and that yearning that must have characterized Merton's secret, unspoken, and unrevealed dialogues with his God.

The personal prayers collected here were born out of Merton's continuous practice of public prayer. His dialogues with God as a

Christian monk were nourished by the psalms, the public prayers of the Jews. He prayed and sang the psalms every day throughout the day for twenty-seven years. Through the words of the Psalter sung in choir with his brothers, he joined himself to the groaning of all creation by the public voicing of its longing, complaint, wonder, trust, and praise at the mysteries of being alive. As a priest he offered Eucharist every day as the center of his day and of his prayer life. His prayers and drawings gathered here are thus best understood as only occasional surfacings from his continuous deep immersion in public worship.

Only once did Merton ever write of his secret way of praying in a letter to a Sufi corresponding with him from Pakistan. To Abdul Aziz he confided,

I have a very simple way of prayer. It is centered entirely on attention to the presence of God and to His will and His love. That is to say it is centered on faith by which alone we can know the presence of God. One might say this gives my meditation the character described by the Prophet as "being before God as if you saw Him." Yet it does not mean imagining anything or conceiving a precise image of God, for to my mind this would be a kind of idolatry. On the contrary, it is a matter of adoring Him as invisible and infinitely beyond our comprehension, and realizing Him as all. My prayer tends very much toward what you call fana. There is in my heart this great thirst to recognize totally the nothingness of all that is not God. My prayer is then a kind of praise rising up out of the center of Nothing and Silence.

This book is a partial harvest from over four hundred prayers collected from all of Merton's published and unpublished works.[1] Merton's line drawings have been selected from a collection of eight hundred drawings archived in the official repository of his work at Bellarmine University's Thomas Merton Center in Louisville, Kentucky. The drawings in this collection are, in the main, representational, and they are mostly from the 1950s. During the 1960s Merton's art would become more calligraphic and abstract and resonate with his interest in Zen and studies of Eastern cultures.

The most powerful and mysterious of the drawings in this book—originating as they do from a monk—are his drawings of women. By temperament Merton was always tempted to go his way alone, an Adam without an Eve to encumber him. These drawings of women reflect his growing appreciation of women and the feminine in his life beyond his early history with women as mere conquests.

In his private journals Merton reveals dreams that are populated with women and feminine imagery. He dreamed of a Chinese princess, who knew and loved him. He dreamed of a black foster mother who had raised him harshly but well and who now danced with him. He dreamed of a young Jewish girl, a recurring dream figure who revealed her name to him as Proverb. Proverb would revisit him again and again in the guise of other women's faces, both in flesh and in dream.

---

[1] The Sources and Notes section at the end of the book identifies each prayer's origin.

This chorus of women's faces, only a small portion of which are gathered in this book, are souvenirs of all the women who companioned this monk's life, feminized his heart's inner ear, and taught him to love and appropriate wisdom as the ground of his own soul. In experiencing the visitations of Proverb, Merton was experiencing the epiphanies of his own secret self—the secret place where God was always abiding within him as an intimate and integrating his fragmented life into a hidden wholeness.

May these prayers and drawings, Thomas Merton's dialogues with silence, be of benefit to all those wise enough to know that they no longer know where they are going. May those who cannot pray and those who still pray but without hope find courage in these pages. May those forced to travel by night take comfort here. May those who yearn for God learn through these pages that God is passionately yearning for them. As we all stumble falteringly forward together through the darkness, may the God who is hurrying toward us, rushing like a mother runs at the sound of cries, find us all quickly.

Jonathan Montaldo
The Thomas Merton Center
April 2001

Vocation to Solitude—To deliver oneself up, to hand oneself over, entrust oneself completely to the silence of a wide landscape of woods and hills, or sea, or desert; to sit still while the sun comes up over the land and fills its silences with light. To pray and work in the morning and to labor in meditation in the evening when night falls upon that land and when the silence fills itself with darkness and with stars. This is a true and special vocation. There are few who are willing to belong completely to such silence, to let it soak into their bones, to breathe nothing but silence, to feed on silence, and to turn the very substance of their life into a living and vigilant silence.

Thoughts in Solitude

Out here in the woods I can think of nothing except God. It is not so much that I think of Him as I am aware of Him as I am of the sun and the clouds and the blue sky and the thin cedar trees. . . . Engulfed in the simple and lucid actuality of the afternoon—I mean God's afternoon—this sacramental moment of time when the shadows will get longer and longer, and one small bird sings quietly in the cedars, one car goes by in the remote distance, and the oak leaves move in the wind.

High up in the summer sky I watch the silent flight of a vulture, and the day goes by in prayer. This solitude confirms my call to solitude. The more I am in it, the more I love it. One day it will possess me entirely and no man will ever see me again.

A Search for Solitude

What I wear is pants. What I do is live. How I pray is breathe.

Day of a Stranger

Lord, when the clock strikes
Telling the time with cold tin
And I sit hooded in this lectern
Waiting for the monks to come,
I see the red cheeses, and bowls
All smile with milk in ranks upon their tables.

Light fills my proper globe
(I have one light to read by
With a little, tinkling chain)

And the monks come down the cloister
With robes as voluble as water.
I do not see them but I hear their waves.

It is winter, and my hands prepare
To turn the pages of the saints:
And to the trees Thy moon has frozen on the windows
My tongue shall sing Thy Scripture.

Then the monks pause upon the step
(With me here in this lectern
And Thee there on Thy crucifix)
And gather little pearls of water on their fingers' ends
Smaller than this my psalm.

Thou Art Not as I Have Conceived Thee

Lord, it is nearly midnight and I am waiting for You in the darkness and the great silence. I am sorry for all my sins. Do not let me ask any more than to sit in the darkness and light no lights of my own, and be crowded with no crowds of my own thoughts to fill the emptiness of the night in which I await You.

In order to remain in the sweet darkness of pure Faith, let me become nothing to the pale, weak light of sense. As to the world, let me become totally obscure from it forever. Thus, through this darkness, may I come to Your brightness at last. Having become insignificant to the world, may I reach out towards the infinite meanings contained in Your peace and Your glory.

Your brightness is my darkness. I know nothing of You and, by myself, I cannot even imagine how to go about knowing You. If I imagine You, I am mistaken. If I understand You, I am deluded. If I am conscious and certain I know You, I am crazy. Darkness is enough.

O flaming Heart,
Unseen and unimagined in this wilderness,
You, You alone are real, and here I've found You.
Here will I love and praise You in a tongueless death,
Until my white devoted bones,
Long bleached and polished by the winds of this Sahara,
Relive at Your command,
Rise and unfold the flowers of their everlasting spring.

Tribulation detaches us from the things of nothingness in which we spend ourselves and die. Therefore, tribulation gives us life and we love it, not out of love for death, but out of love for life.

Let me then withdraw all my love from scattered, vain things—the desire to be read and praised as a writer, to be a successful teacher praised by my students, or to live at ease in some beautiful place—and let me place everything in Thee, where it will take root and live, instead of being spent in barrenness.

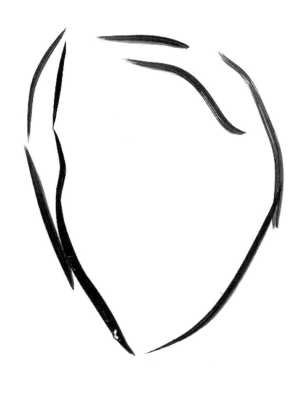

O God, my God, why am I so mute? I long to cry out and out to Thee, over and over, and Thou art nameless and infinite. All our names for Thee are not Thy name, infinite Trinity. But Thy Word is Jesus and I cry the name of Thy Son and live in the love of His heart and believe, if He wills, that He will bring me the answer to my only prayer: that I may renounce *everything* and belong entirely to the Lord!

In one sense we are always traveling, and traveling as if we did not know where we were going.

In another sense we have already arrived.

We cannot arrive at the perfect possession of God in this life, and that is why we are traveling and in darkness. But we already possess Him by grace, and therefore, in that sense, we have arrived and are dwelling in the light.

But oh! How far have I to go to find You in Whom I have already arrived!

My God, it is to You alone that I can talk because nobody else will understand. I cannot bring anyone on this earth into the cloud where I dwell in Your light—that is, in Your darkness where I am lost and abashed. I cannot explain to anyone the anguish which is Your joy, nor the loss which is the possession of You, nor the distance from all things which is the arrival in You, nor the death which is the birth in You, because I do not know anything about it myself. All I know is that I wish it were over—I wish it were begun.

You have contradicted everything. You have left me in no-man's land.

You have got me walking up and down all day under those trees, saying to me over and over again: "Solitude, solitude." And You have turned around and thrown the whole world in my lap. You have told me, "Leave all things and follow me," and then You have tied half of New York to my foot like a ball and chain. You have got me kneeling behind that pillar with my mind making a noise like a bank. Is that contemplation?

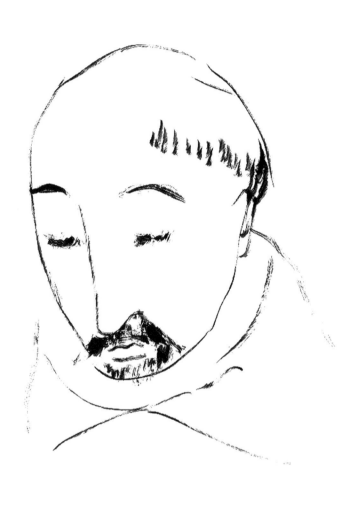

My God, I frankly do not understand Your ways with me. You fill me with desires that people have been canonized for having and for carrying out. Then You tell me not to carry them out, and You tell me in such a way that it would seem to be a sin if I carried them out. Then You make the desires grow more and more until they consume the very foundations of my life. Are You trying to kill me?

You have shown me the great quiet mountains, the silent cells where Your solitaries dwell hidden in the secret of Your Face, forgotten by everyone, living in You alone, without speech, buried in the darkness of faith, not lost in useless arts, or the bewilderment of business, their lives uncluttered by the fruitless drives and preoccupations of those who still seek You in the smoke of their own deeds, of their own activity. You have told me: "This is the best part, they have chosen it, and it shall not be taken from them."

But if I try to choose it, too, You take it from me and say: "Go here, go there; do this, and do that. Never be alone. Have your mind full of preoccupations and your heart tangled with temporal things." Can it be that You will these things?

The months have gone by, and You have given me peace, and I am beginning to see what it is all about. I am beginning to understand.

You have called me to Gethsemani not to wear a label by which I can recognize myself and place myself in some kind of a category. You do not want me to be thinking about what I am, but about what You are. Or rather, You do not even want me to be thinking about anything much: for You would raise me above the level of thought. If I am always trying to figure out what I am and where I am and why I am, how will that work be done?

I do not make a big drama of this business. I do not say: "You have asked me for everything, and I have renounced all." I no longer desire to see anything that implies a distance between You and me. If I stand back and consider myself and You, as if something had passed between us, from me to You, I will inevitably see the gap between us and remember the distance between us.

My God, it is that gap and that distance which kill me.

That is the only reason why I desire solitude—to be lost to all created things, to die to them, to the knowledge of them, for they remind me of my distance from You. They tell me something about You: that You are far from them, even though You are in them. You have made them and Your presence sustains their being, but they hide You from me. And I would live alone, and out of them. *O beata solitudo, O blessed solitude!*

For I knew that it was only by leaving them that I could come to You: and that is why I have been so unhappy when You seemed to be condemning me to remain in them. Now my sorrow is over and my joy is about to begin: the joy that rejoices in the deepest sorrows. For I am beginning to understand. You have taught me and have consoled me, and I have begun again to hope and learn.

I will travel to You, Lord, through a thousand blind alleys. You want to bring me to You through stone walls.

O Lord, how joyful and happy must they be who, when they come to consider their own selves, find in themselves nothing remarkable whatever. Not only do they not attract attention outside themselves, but now they no longer have any desires or selfish interests to attract their own attention. They remark no virtues; they are saddened by no huge sins; they see only their own unremarkable weakness and nothingness but a nothingness that is filled obscurely, not with themselves, but with Your love, O God! They are poor in spirit who possess within themselves the kingdom of heaven because they are no longer remarkable even to themselves. But in them shines God's light and they themselves, and all who see it, glorify You, O God!

The Holy Spirit, Who is Love living in me, is the One Who brought this day of my Solemn Profession as a monk about. The Holy Spirit is preparing far more surprising things in the future, if I will let Him act.

There is nothing else worth living for: only this infinitely peaceful Love Who is beyond words, beyond emotion, beyond intelligence.

Cradle me, Holy Spirit, in Your dark silver cloud and protect me against the heat of my own speech, my own judgments, and my own vision. Ward off the sickness of consolation and desire, of fear and grief that spring from desire. I will give You my will for You to cleanse and rinse of all this clay.

Tomorrow, having commended to You the needs and intentions of everybody in the world and in the Church, the needs of contemplatives and of my friends and of all whom I have ever known, I want to give myself to You without solicitude, without fear or desire, not seeking words or silence, work or rest, light or darkness, company or solitude. For I will possess all things if I am empty of all things, and only You can at once empty me of all things and fill me with Yourself, the Life of all that lives, and the Being in Whom everything exists.

This will be my solitude, to be separated from myself so that I am able to love You alone, to love You so much that I no longer realize I am loving anything. For such a realization implies a consciousness of a self that is separated from You. I no longer desire to be myself, but to find myself transformed in You, so that there is no "myself" but only Yourself. That is when I will be what You have willed to make me from all eternity: not myself, but Love. Thus will be fulfilled in me, as You will it to be fulfilled, Your reason for the creation of the world and of me in it.

O my God, I don't care about anything; all I know is that I want to love You. I want my will to disappear in Your will. I want to be one spirit with You. I want to become all Your desires and thoughts. I want to live in the middle of Your Trinity and praise You with the flames of Your own praise. O my God, knowing all this, why do You leave me alone in my selfishness and in my vanity and pride, instead of drawing me into the midst of Your love? My God, do not delay any longer to make me a saint and to make me one with You, and do not delay to live in me. And if it requires sacrifice, You will give me the courage to make all sacrifices. You will consume me in Your own immense love. So do not be afraid of my weakness, O God, because You can do everything. I believe in Your love above all things. I have forgotten everything else (that is, I want to). I live for Your love, if You will only make me live so.

All day I have waited for You with my faculties still bleeding the poison of their suppressed activity. I have waited for Your silence and Your peace to staunch and cleanse them, O my Lord.

You will heal me when You will, because I have trusted in You.

I will not wound myself anymore with details with which I have surrounded myself like thorns—a penance that You do not desire of me.

You have made my soul for Your peace and Your silence and my soul is wounded with confusion, with the noise of my sins and my desires.

I am made for Your peace and You will not despise my longing to love You alone in this sorrow because I have trusted in You and I wait upon Your holy will in peace and without complaint for Your glory.

I am content that these journal pages show me to be what I am: noisy, full of the racket of imperfections and passions and the wide open wounds left by sin, full of faults and envies and miseries, full of my own intolerable emptiness.

Domine Deus Meus in te confido; non confundar in aeternum. Lord, My God, in You I trust. Let me not be put to shame forever.

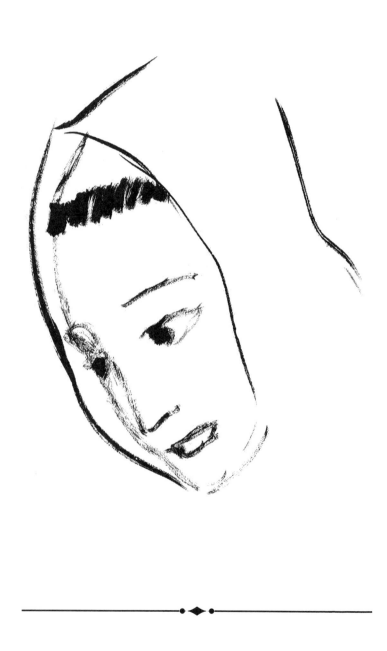

When all the monks come in with eyes as clean as the
    cold sky
And axes under their arms,
Still praying out *Ave Marias,*
With rosaries between their bleeding fingers,
We shake the chips out of our robes outside the door
And go to hide in cowls as deep as clouds,
Bowing our shoulders in the church's shadow, lean
And whipped,
To wait upon your Vespers, Mother of God!

My God, I give up my attachment to peace, the delight and sweetness of contemplation, of Your love and Your presence. I give myself to You to love Your will and Your honor alone.

I know that, if You want me to renounce the manner of my desiring You, it is only in order that I may possess You surely and come to union with You.

I will try from now on, with Your grace, to make no more fuss about "being a contemplative," about acquiring that perfection for myself. Instead I will seek only You, not contemplation and not perfection, but You alone.

Then maybe I will be able to do the simple things that You would have me do, and do them well, with a perfect and pure intention in all peace and silence and obscurity, concealed even from my own self, and safe from my poisonous self-esteem.

All I want, Jesus, is more and more to abandon everything to You. The more I go on, the more I realize I don't know where I am going. Lead me and take complete control of me.

Doce me facere voluntatem tuam quia Deus meus es tu. Teach me to do thy will, for You are my God.

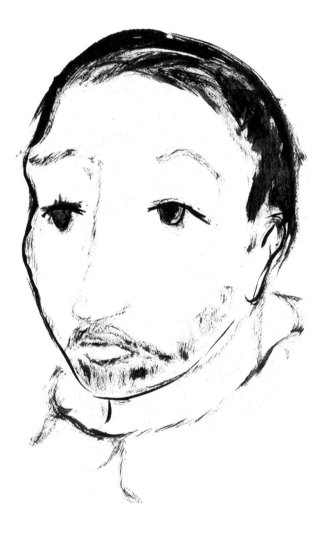

My God, lock me in Your Will, imprison me in Your Love and Your Wisdom, draw me to Yourself. I will never do anything when the strongest reason for doing it is only my own satisfaction. I want Your Will and Your Love. I give myself blindly to You. I trust in You. Do You really want me in solitude? Then lead me there and purify the way of all my own will and of my own desires. I trust in You blindly. I will keep close to You whatever the darkness, whatever my fears may be. Lead me to do all things in Your own time and in Your own way.

You know my soul. You know all that needs to be done there. Do it in Your own way. Draw me to You, O my God. Fill me with Pure Love of You alone. Make me never go aside from the way of Your Love. Show me clearly that way and never let me depart from it: that will be enough. I leave everything in Your hands. You will guide me without error and without danger and I will love You all the way. I will belong to You. I will not be afraid of anything for I shall remain in Your hands and never leave You.

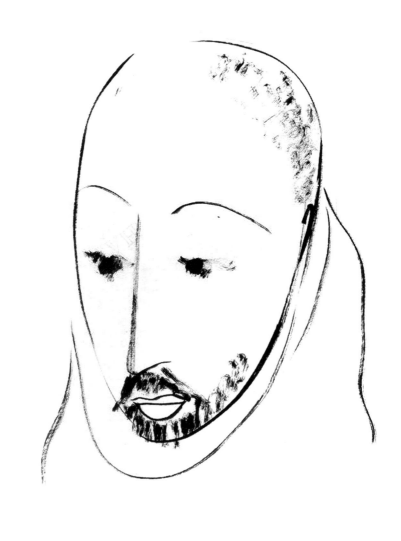

What can I say about the emptiness and freedom into whose door I entered for that half-minute, which was enough for a lifetime, because it was a new life altogether? There is nothing with which to compare it. I could call it nothingness, but it is an infinitely fruitful freedom, to lack all things and to lack my self in the fresh air of that happiness that seems to be above all modes of being. Don't let me build any more walls around it, or I will shut myself out.

When will You come back? Tomorrow on the Feast of Christ the King?

It seems to me that I should never desire anything but this pure love of You which is You loving Yourself, not only in my soul, but in all my faculties so that they are empty and lost and finished and done with and nothing is left but liberty.

Now at last let me begin to live by faith. *Quaerite primum regnum Dei. Seek first the kingdom of God.* Why do I mistrust Your goodness, mistrust everyone but myself, meet every new event on the defensive, squared off against everybody?

Dear Lord, I am not living like a monk, like a contemplative. The first essential is missing. I only say I trust You. My actions prove that the one I trust is myself—and that I am still afraid of You.

Take my life into Your hands at last. Do whatever You want with it. I give myself to Your love. I mean to keep on giving myself to Your love—rejecting neither the hard things nor the pleasant things You have arranged for me. It is enough for me that You have glory. Everything You have planned is good. It is all love.

The way You have laid open before me is an easy way, compared with the hard way of my own will which leads back to Egypt and to bricks without straw.

If You allow people to praise me, I shall not worry. If You let them blame me, I shall worry even less. If You send me work, I shall embrace it with joy. It will be rest to me because it is Your will. If You send me rest, I will rest in You. Only save me from myself. Save me from my own, private, poisonous urge to change everything, to act without reason, to move for movement's sake, to unsettle everything that You have ordained.

Let me rest in Your will and be silent. Then the light of Your joy will warm my life. Its fire will burn in my heart and shine for Your glory. This is what I live for. Amen, amen.

St John
Baptist

Bring me with joy, God, across Thy Jordan. I am sorry I forget my desires and burn with other desires to complete my work, to get books distributed to people. But there is only one desire: to find the promised land and the freedom of a pure love that is without concern for anything else but love—that is, without concern for anything but the purity of God, for His will, His glory. Let me be brought to a peace above language, not in some esoteric *state*, but in the living reality of a love that is contemplation and act, that clings to God and embraces all the world in Him in peace, in unity.

My God, I pray better to You by breathing.
I pray better to You by walking than by talking.

Lord Jesus Christ, true God and true Man, in Whom the fullness of God dwells and is manifested, whoever tries to be a contemplative without You is dead. Whoever enters into interior darkness in which You cannot be found enters into the gate of hell. Whoever enters into a silence in which Your voice cannot be heard enters into the antechamber of the devil. Whoever goes where You cannot be seen is crazy.

I will not fear the darkness where, desiring to find You, my desire does not seem to find You. But if I desire You, I have already found You. If I love You, You are with me. If I cry out to You, You have already heard my voice.

O God, teach me to be satisfied with my own helplessness in the spiritual life. Teach me to be content with Your grace that comes to me in darkness and that works things I cannot see. Teach me to be happy that I can depend on You. To depend on You should be enough for an eternity of joy. To depend on You by itself ought to be infinitely greater than any joy which my own intellectual appetite could desire.

I listen to the clock tick. Downstairs the thermostat has just stopped humming. God is in this room. He is in my heart. So much so that it is difficult to read or write. Nevertheless, I'll get busy on the Book of Isaias which is Your word, O my God. May Your fire grow in me and may I find You in Your beautiful fire. It is very quiet, O my God. Your moon shines on our hills. Your moonlight shines in my wide-open soul when everything is silent. *Adolezco peno y muero. I languish, suffer and die* (John of the Cross).

Our Eden is the heart of Christ.

Let grace come, Jesus.
Your name is on my heart.
Your Holy Name is on the tower of my heart.
Let grace come and let this world pass away,
Jesus, You Who are living in my exhausted heart.

On this gray morning, when the birds sing in the rain, I proclaim that there is a sad note to our spring. We lift up our eyes to You in heaven, O God of eternity, wishing we were poorer, more silent and more mortified. Lord, give us liberty from all things that are in this world, from the preoccupations of earth and of time, that we may be called to cleanness where the saints are, the gold and silver saints before Your throne.

How lovely are thy tabernacles, O Lord of hosts! The sparrow hath found herself a house and the turtle dove a nest for herself where she may lay her little ones.

This Gethsemani is the land where You have given me roots in eternity, O God of heaven and earth. This is the burning promised land, the house of God, the gate of heaven, the place of peace, the place of silence, the place of wrestling with the angel.

Blessed are they who dwell in thy house, O Lord! They shall praise Thee forever and ever.

I pray over and over—make me love You, Lord, and Mary, our Mother, make me love and love. I am no longer scared to say it over and over. How can I love You? Not only by kneeling and saying over and over I love You for the goodness of all things, and thanking You for the being of all things, especially my own, but by praying to be able to thank You more humbly and with more love. Why should I pray for love except in order to thank You more lovingly for all Your sweet creation? If I pray for love so as to have love and enjoy it, I lose it at once. Only if I ask for enough love to give back to You (because in my own complete poverty I have nothing I can give) is the prayer answered, full of grace, so that I want nothing more but only to stay here praying for more love to give back.

Prayers on the Fire Watch, July 4, 1952

The night, O my Lord, is a time of freedom.

You have seen the morning and the night, and the night was better. In the night all things began, and in the night the end of all things has come before me.

In the night I have spoken to You on the roof of the house that shall one day perish.

God, my God, God Whom I meet in darkness, with You it is always the same thing! Always the same question that nobody knows how to answer!

I have prayed to You in the daytime with thoughts and reasons, and in the nighttime You have confronted me, scattering thought and reason. I have come to You in the morning light and with desire, and You have descended upon me with great gentleness, with most forbearing silence in this inexplicable night, dispersing light, defeating all desire. I have explained to You a hundred times my motives for entering the monastery, and You have listened and said nothing, and I have turned away and wept with shame.

Is it true that my motives have meant nothing? Is it true that all my desires were an illusion?

While I am asking questions that You do not answer, You ask me a question that is so simple that I cannot answer it. I do not even understand the question.

This night, and every night, it is the same question.

Here, now, by night, with this huge clock ticking on my right hip and the flashlight in my hand and my sneakers on my feet, I feel as if everything has been unreal. It is as if the past had never existed. The things I thought were so important—because of the effort I put into them—have turned out to be of small value. The things I never thought about, the things I was never able either to measure or to expect, they were the things that mattered.

But in this darkness I would not be able to say, for certain, what it was that mattered. That, perhaps, is part of Your unanswerable question!

This nearness to You in the darkness is too simple and too close for excitement. It is commonplace for all things to live an unexpected life in the night: but their life is illusory and unreal. The illusion of sound only intensifies the infinite substance of Your silence.

Here at Gethsemani, in this place where I made my vows, where I have had my hands anointed for the Holy Sacrifice, where I have had Your priesthood seal the depth and intimate summit of my being, a word, a thought, would defile the quiet of Your inexplicable love.

Your Love, O God, speaks to my life as to an intimate in the midst of a crowd of strangers: I mean these walls, this roof, these arches, this (overhead), ridiculously large and unsubstantial tower.

Lord God, the whole world tonight seems made out of paper. The most substantial things are ready to crumble apart and blow away.

How much more so this monastery which everybody believes in and which has perhaps ceased to exist?

O God, my God, the night has values that the day has never dreamed of.

---◆---

Now is the time to get up and go to the tower. Now is the time to meet You, God, where the night is wonderful, where the roof is almost without substance under my feet, where all the mysterious junk in the belfry scorns the proximate coming of three new bells, where the forest opens out under the moon, and the living things sing terribly that only the present is eternal and that all things having a past and a future are doomed to pass away.

Lord God of this great night, do You see the woods? Do You hear the rumor of their loneliness? Do You behold their secrecy? Do You remember their solitudes? Do You see that my soul is beginning to dissolve like wax within me?

Deus meus clamabo per diem, et non exaudies; et nocte, et non ad insipientiam mihi. My God, I cry out by day but You do not hear me; at night, but You give me no relief! Do You remember the place by the stream? Do You remember the top of the Vineyard Knob that time in autumn when the train was in the valley? Do You remember McGinty's hollow? Do You remember the thinly wooded hillside behind Hanekamp's place? Do You remember the time of the forest fire? Do You know what has become of the little poplars we planted in the spring? Do You observe the valley where I marked the trees?

There is no leaf that is not in Your care. There is no cry that was not heard by You before it was uttered. There is no water in the shales that was not hidden there by Your wisdom. There is no concealed spring that was not concealed by You. There is no glen for a lone house that was not planned by You for a lone house. There is no man for that acre of woods that was not made by You for that acre of woods.

But there is a greater comfort in the substance of silence than in the answer to a question. Eternity is in the present. Eternity is in the palm of the hand. Eternity is a seed of fire whose sudden roots break barriers that keep my heart from being an abyss.

The things of Time are in connivance with eternity. The shadows serve You. The beasts sing to You before they pass away. The solid hills shall vanish like a worn out garment. All things change and die and disappear. Questions arrive, assume their actuality, and disappear. In this hour I shall cease to ask them and silence shall be my answer. The world that Your love created, that the heat has distorted, that my mind is always misinterpreting, shall cease to interfere with our voices.

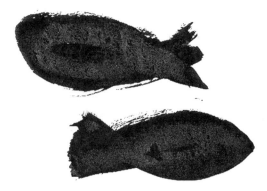

Minds which are separated pretend to blend in one another's
language. The marriage of souls in concepts is mostly an
illusion. Thoughts which travel outward bring back reports
from You from outward things, but a dialogue with You,
uttered through the world, always ends by being a dialogue
with my own reflection in the stream of time. With You there
is no dialogue, unless You choose a mountain, circle it with
cloud and print Your words in fire upon the mind of Moses.
What was delivered to Moses on tablets of stone, as the fruit of
lightning and thunder, is now more thoroughly born in our
souls as quietly as the breath of our own being.

You Who sleep in my breast are not met with words, but in the emergence of life within life and of wisdom within wisdom. With You there is no longer any dialogue, any contest, any opposition. You are found in communion! Thou in me and I in Thee, Thou in them and they in me: dispossession within dispossession, dispassion within dispassion, emptiness within emptiness, freedom within freedom. I am alone. Thou art alone. The Father and I are One.

What is easier than to discuss mutually with You, O God, the three crows that flew by in the sun with light flashing on their rubber wings? Or the sunlight coming quietly through the cracks in the boards? Or the crickets in the grass? You are sanctified in them when, beyond the blue hills, my mind is lost in Your intentions for us all who live with hope under the servitude of corruption!

You have called me into this silence to be grateful for what silence I have and to use it by desiring more.

Heaven and earth are full of Thy glory and Thy mercy. I who am nothing have been placed here in silence to behold Thy glory and mercy and to praise Thee!

I am grateful to my students simply because they exist and because they are what they are. I am grateful to You, O God, for having placed me among them and for having told me to be their father. But finally, I am grateful to You, O God, because I am now more often alone. Not that I run away from my students, yet sometimes I do not know myself in them. At other times I find myself in them and with them. Indeed, spiritual direction is sometimes an experiment in recognition: they recognize something new in themselves and I in myself: for You, O God, recognize Yourself in us.

Do you suppose I have a spiritual life? I have none. I am indigence. I am silence. I am poverty. I am solitude, for I have renounced spirituality to find God, and He it is Who preaches loudly in the depths of my indigence saying: "I will pour out my spirit upon thy children and they shall spring up among the herbs as willows beside the running waters" (Isaias 44:3–4). "The children of thy barrenness shall say in thy ears: 'The place is too strait for me, make me room to dwell in'" (Isaias 49:20). I die of love for you, Compassion: I take you for my Lady, as Francis married poverty, I marry you, the Queen of hermits and the Mother of the poor.

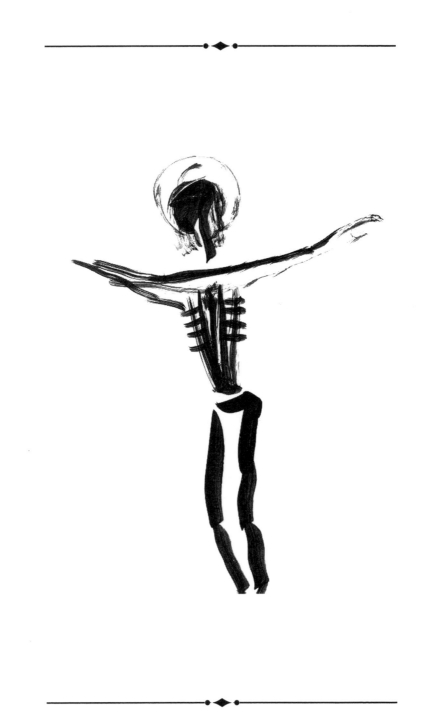

O Lord my God, where have I been sleeping? What have I been doing? How slowly I awaken once again to the barrenness of my life and its confusion. You will forgive me if it is often that way—I do not mean it to be. How little faith there has been in me—how inert have been my hours of solitude, how my time has been wasted. You will forgive me if next week, too, my time is all wasted and I am once again in confusion. But at least this afternoon, sitting on a boulder among the birches, I thought with compunction of Your love and Your kingdom. And again tonight, by the gatehouse, I thought of the hope You have planted in our hearts and of the Kingdom of Heaven that I have done so little to gain for myself and for others.

Forgive me, O Lord, by Your Cross and Passion and Resurrection. Teach me to see what it means that I am saved by Your Church. Teach me how, as a priest, I am to bring others to the knowledge of You and of the Kingdom and to salvation. Teach me to live in You with care for the purity of faith, with the zeal of true hope, and with true and objective charity for my brothers, for the glory of the Father, Amen.

God, have mercy on me in the blindness in which I hope I am seeking You!

My Lord, You have heard the cry of my heart because it was You Who cried out within my heart.

Forgive me for having tried to evoke Your presence in my own silence. It is You Who must create me within Your own silence! Only this newness can save me from idolatry!

You are not found in the Temple merely by the expulsion of the moneychangers.

You are not found on the mountain every time there is a cloud. The earth swallowed those who offered incense without having been found, without having been called, and without having been known by You.

My Lord, I have no hope but in Your Cross. You, by Your humility, sufferings and death, have delivered me from all vain hope. You have killed the vanity of the present life in Yourself and have given me all that is eternal in rising from the dead.

My hope is in what the eye has never seen. Therefore let me not trust in visible rewards. My hope is in what the human heart cannot feel. Therefore let me not trust in the feelings of my heart. My hope is in what the hand has never touched. Do not let me trust what I can grasp between my fingers, because Death will loosen my grasp and my vain hope will be gone.

Let my trust be in Your mercy, not in myself. Let my hope be in Your love, not in health or strength or ability or human resources.

If I trust You, everything else will become for me strength, health and support. Everything will bring me to heaven. If I do not trust You, everything will be my destruction.

O great God, Father of all things, whose infinite light is darkness to me, Whose immensity is to me as the Void, You have called me forth out of Yourself because You love me in Yourself. I am a transient expression of Your inexhaustible and eternal reality. I could not know You, I would be lost in this darkness, I would fall away for You into this Void, if You did not hold me to Yourself in the Heart of Your only begotten Son.

Father, I love You Whom I do not know. I embrace You Whom I do not see. I abandon myself to You Whom I have offended. You love in me Your only begotten Son. You see Him in me. You embrace Him in me, because He has willed to identify Himself completely with me by that love which brought Him to death, for me, on the Cross.

I come to You like Jacob in the garments of Esau—that is, in the merits and the Precious Blood of Jesus Christ. You, Father, Who have willed to be as though blind in the darkness of this great mystery that is the revelation of Your love, pass Your hands over my head and bless me as Your only Son. You have willed to see me only in Him, but, willing this, You have willed to see me more really as I am. For my sinful self is not my real self, it is not the self You have wanted for me, only the self that I have wanted for myself. I no longer want this false self. And now, Father, I come to You in Your own Son's self, for it is His Sacred Heart that has taken possession of me and destroyed my sins and it is He who presents me to You. Where? In the sanctuary of His own Heart which is Your palace, the temple where the saints adore You in heaven.

Let this be my only consolation—that, wherever I am, You my Lord are loved and praised.

The trees indeed love You without knowing You. Without being aware of Your presence, the tiger lilies and cornflowers proclaim that they love You. The beautiful dark clouds ride slowly across the sky musing on You like children who do not know what they are dreaming of as they play.

In the midst of them all, I know You and I know of Your Presence. In them and in me I know of the love that they do not know and, what is greater, I am abashed by the presence of Your love in me. O kind and terrible love which You have given me and which could never be in my heart if You did not love me! In the midst of these beings that have never offended You, I am loved by You, most of all as one who has offended You. I am seen by You under the sky and my offenses have been forgotten by You.

In solitude I have at last discovered that You desire the love of my heart, O my God, the love of my heart as it is—the love of my human heart. I have found and have known by Your great mercy that the love of a heart that is abandoned and broken and poor is most pleasing to You and attracts the gaze of Your pity. It is Your desire and Your consolation, O my Lord, to be very close to those who love You and call upon You as their Father. You have perhaps no greater *consolation*—if I may so speak—than to console Your afflicted children and those who come to You poor and empty handed, with nothing but their humanness, their limitations and their great trust in Your mercy.

My Father, I know You have called me to live alone with You and to learn that, if I were not a mere human being capable of mistakes and evil, capable of a frail and errant human affection for You, I would not be capable of being Your child. You desire the love of my heart because Your Divine Son also loves You with a human heart. He became a human being in order that my heart and His heart should love You in one love, which is a human love born and moved by Your Holy Spirit.

If therefore I do not love You with a human love and with a human simplicity, and with the humility to be myself, I will never taste the full sweetness of Your Fatherly mercy, and Your Son, as far as my life goes, will have died in vain.

Lord, have mercy.

Have mercy on my darkness, my weakness, my confusion. Have mercy on my infidelity, my cowardice, my turning about in circles, my wandering, my evasions.

I do not ask anything but such mercy, always, in everything, mercy. My life here at Gethsemani—a little solidity and very much ashes.

Almost everything is ashes. What I have prized most is ashes. What I have attended to least is, perhaps, a little solid.

Lord have mercy. Guide me, make me want again to be holy, to be a man of God even though in desperateness and confusion.

I do not necessarily ask for clarity, a plain way, but only to go according to Your love, to follow Your mercy, to trust in Your mercy.

A Prayer to God My Father on the Vigil of Pentecost

Today, Father, this blue sky praises You. The delicate green and orange flowers of the tulip poplar praise You. The distant blue hills praise You together with the sweet smelling air that is full of brilliant light. The bickering flycatchers praise You with the lowing cattle and the quails that whistle over there. I, too, Father, praise You with these creatures, my brothers and sisters. You have made us all together and You have placed me here this morning in the midst of them. And here I am.

I prayed for a long time in the years that are past, and I was in darkness and sorrow and confusion. No doubt the confusion was my own fault. No doubt my own will was the root of my sorrow. I regret it, O merciful Father. But whatever may have been my sin, the prayer of Your friends for me and my own prayers were answered because I am here in this hermitage before You. Here You see me. Here You love me. Here You ask the response of my love and confidence. Here You ask me to be nothing else than Your friend.

You have called me here in solitude to be Your son: to be born over again repeatedly in Your light, into knowledge, into consideration, into gratitude and poverty, and into praise.

Here in this hermitage I will learn from the words of Your friends to be Your friend and here I will be a friend to those in whom You send me Your Son.

If I have any choice to make, it is to live and even die here. But in any case, it is to speak Your name with confidence here in this place, to say it by being here and by having You in my heart, as long as I can be here.

Father, I beg You to teach me to be a man of peace and to help bring peace to the world, to study here truth and non-violence, and to have the patience and courage to suffer for truth.

Send me Your Holy Spirit, unite me with Your divine Son, make me one with You in Him, for Your great glory. Amen.

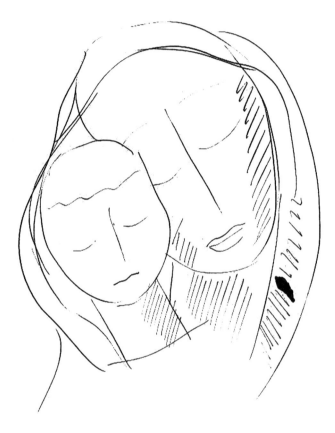

Christ, from my cradle I had known You everywhere,
And even though I sinned, I walked in You, and knew
You were my world:
You were my France and England,
My seas and my America:
You were my life and air.

Lady, the night has got us by the heart.
The whole wide world is tumbling down.
Words turn to ice in my dry throat
Praying for a land without prayer,

Walking to you on water all winter
In a year that wants more war.

Lady, when on that night I left the Island that was once your England, your love went with me, although I could not know it, and could not make myself aware of it. It was your love, your intercession for me before God, that was preparing the seas before my ship, laying open the way for me to another country.

I was not sure where I was going and I could not see what I would do when I got to New York. But you saw further and clearer than I and you opened the seas before my ship whose track led me across the waters to a place I had never dreamed of, and which you were even then preparing for me to be my rescue and my shelter and my home. And when I thought there was no God and no love and no mercy, you were leading me all the while into the midst of His love and His mercy and taking me, without my knowing anything about it, to the house that would hide me in the secret of His Face.

When we had crossed over the divide and were going down through the green valleys towards the Caribbean Sea, I saw the yellow Basilica of Our Lady of Cobre standing on a rising above the tin roofs of the mining village in the depths of a deep bowl of green, backed by cliffs and sheer slopes robed in jungle.

There you are, Caridad del Cobre! It is you that I have come to see. You will ask Christ to make me His priest and I will give you my heart, Lady. And if you will obtain for me this priesthood, I will remember you at my first Mass in such a way that the Mass will be for you and offered through your hands in gratitude to the Holy Trinity Who has used your love to win me this great grace.

Lady, Queen of Heaven, pray me into solitude and silence and unity, that all my ways may be immaculate in God. Let me be content with whatever darkness surrounds me, finding Him always by me, in His Mercy. Let me keep silence in this world, except in so far as God wills and in the way He wills it. Let me at least disappear into the writing I do. It should mean nothing special to me, nor harm my recollection. The work could be a prayer; its results should not concern me.

La Soledad! Lady of Solitude! My whole interior life is summed up in you.

No need to talk about it; to live it is to console you. I must empty myself of all things so as to be poor and desolate with you. I look for you in your almost impenetrable solitude. Your loneliness is all my friendship. Your desolation becomes my life.

Haec requies mea in saeculum saeculi. This is my rest forever and ever: to seek to console you by having Christ living in me, for He is my love for you.

He is the one who burns my heart for you, *Soledad!*
Ave Maria!
Soledad, I love you.

A Prayer to Our Lady of Mount Carmel

What was it that I said to you, in the mirror, at Havana?

Were you not perhaps the last one I saw, as the steamer left, and you were standing on your tower with your back to the sea, looking at the university?

I have never forgotten you. And you are more to me now than then, when I walked through the streets reciting (which I had just learned) that prayer to you, the *Memorare:*

[Remember, O most gracious Virgin Mary, that never was it known that anyone who fled to thy protection, implored thy help, or sought thy intercession was left unaided. Inspired by this confidence I fly unto thee, O Virgin of Virgins, my Mother. To thee I come, before thee I stand, sinful and sorrowful. O Mother of the Word Incarnate, despise not my petitions, but in thy mercy hear and answer me. Amen.]

I have forgotten all the things I have prayed for to you. I think I have received them, but I do not remember, but more importantly I have received you.

Whom I know and yet do not know. Whom I love but not enough.

Prayer is what you bring—for prayer is your gift to us, not what you ask of us.

Teach me to go to this country beyond words and beyond names.

Teach me to pray on this side of the frontier, here where these woods are.

I need to be led by you. I need my heart to be moved by you. I need my soul to be made clean by your prayer. I need my will to be made strong by you. I need the world to be saved and changed by you. I need you for all those who suffer, who are in prison, in danger, in sorrow. I need you for all the crazy people. I need your healing hand to work always in my life. I need you to make me, as you made your Son, a healer, a comforter, a savior. I need you to name the dead. I need you to help the dying cross their particular rivers. I need you for myself whether I live or die. I need to be your monk and your son. It is necessary. Amen.

Lady, to you God has given the mission of bringing us to union, *ut per unam feminam reformemur ad Sapientiam, so that through one woman we may be reformed unto Wisdom.* Through you I can come to solitude to be alone with God. *Coeli finestra facta es. You have been made the window of heaven.*

This is how everything stands, Mother of God, after the First Vespers of Your Nativity in the year 1947. *Dona nobis pacem. Give us peace.* Keep us in your heart until next year and the year after, until we die in peace, disposed in the four corners of America in new monastic foundations, me writing less for magazines, being more silent, perhaps in a cell, all alone with you and God. His will is my cell. His love is my solitude. *Dona nobis pacem. Give us peace.*

Late afternoon. The quiet of the afternoon is filled with an altogether different tonality. The sun has moved altogether around and the room is darker. It is serious. The hour is more weary. I take time out to pray and I look at the picture of the Annunciation by Fra Angelico on a postcard, feeling like the end of Advent, which is today. *Ecce completa sunt omnia quae dicta sunt per angelum de Virgine Maria. Behold all things are fulfilled which the angel spoke about the Virgin Mary*—that was the antiphon after the *Benedictus* this morning. For about eight minutes I stayed silent and did not move and listened to my watch and wondered if perhaps I might not understand something of the work Our Lady is preparing. It is an hour of tremendous expectation.

I remember my weariness, my fears, my lack of understanding, my dimness, my sin of over-activity. What is she preparing: have I offended her? What is coming up? She loves me. I reject emotion about it. Her love is too tremendously serious for any emotion of which I might be capable. Her love shapes worlds, shapes history, forms an Apocalypse in me and around me: gives birth to the City of God. I am drawn back again into where Angelico's angel speaks to her. Fra Angelico knew how to paint her. She is thin, immeasurably noble, and she does not rise to meet the angel. I have here what is said to be a relic of her veil. Mother, make me as sincere as this picture. All the way down into my soul sincere. Let me have no thought that could not kneel before you in that picture. I will act like the picture. *Ecce completa sunt. Behold everything is brought to an end.* It is the end of Advent and the afternoon is vivid with expectancy.

I asked you for peace last winter and there are saints somewhere asking you, Lady, for peace this winter, and so I join my prayers to theirs.

I could say I give myself to you, that I consecrate myself to you, but I have said it all before. Now I mean it more than before, only I can't think of a strong word. Lady, I have written too much and I am not as good at words as a writer ought to be. When I talk to you, the deep things I ought to say simply leave me inarticulate. But anyway, I can say I love you not by spectacular speeches and gestures, but by being a poor, plain Trappist, obscure, more or less stupid, not notable for anything. Never mind. My turn will come soon and I will be left in a corner like everybody else.

Mary ever Virgin, Mother of God our Savior, I entrust myself entirely to your loving intercession and care because you are my Mother and I am your dear child, full of trouble, conflict, error, confusion and prone to sin.

My whole life must change, but because I can do nothing to change it by my own powers, I entrust it with all my needs and cares to you. Present me with pure hands to your Divine Son. Pray that I may gladly accept all that is needed to strip me of myself and become His true disciple, forgetting myself and loving His kingdom, His truth, and all whom He came to save by His Holy Cross. Amen.

I really need prayer in sorrow of heart,
more humble thought of how to go about saying
and doing what I say and do.
I try to act as if I were wise
But I do not have the fear of God without which
there is no beginning of wisdom.
I pray for mercy, but coldly.
What will become of me?
Mother of Mercy and Wisdom,
Take pity on me a sinner.

Glorious Mother of God, shall I ever again distrust you or your God before Whose throne you are irresistible in your intercession? Shall I ever turn my eyes from your hands, from your face or from your eyes? Shall I ever look anywhere else but in the face of your love to find out true counsel and to know my way in all the days and all the moments of my life?

As you have dealt with me, Lady, deal also with all my millions of brothers and sisters who live in the same misery that I knew then. Lead them in spite of themselves and guide them by your tremendous influence, O Holy Queen of Souls and Refuge of Sinners. Bring them to your Christ the way that you brought me. *Illos tuos misericordes oculos ad nos converte, et Jesum, benedictum fructum ventris tui, nobis ostende. Turn your eyes of mercy toward us now and show us Jesus, the blessed fruit of your womb.*

Show us your Christ, Lady, after this our exile, yes, but show Him to us also now, show Him to us here, while we are still wanderers.

A Prayer to Robert Lax

Lax, when you say your prayers, pray for me to be a good priest. Pray for all priests to be good, and pray for the salvation of all people, nuns, business men, Hitler, everybody.

A Prayer to Dorothy Day

O Dorothy, I think of you and the beat people and the ones
with nothing and the poor in virtue, the very poor, the ones no
one can respect. I am not worthy to say I love all of you.
Intercede for me, a stuffed shirt in a place of stuffed shirts and
a big dumb phony, who has tried to be respectable and has
succeeded. What a deception! I know, of course, that you are
respected, too, but you have a right to be. You didn't jump into
the most respectable possible situation and then tell everyone
about it. I am worried about all this, but I am not beating
myself over the head. I just think that, for the love of God,
I should say it, and that, for the love of God, you should
pray for me.

A Prayer to Etienne Gilson

Please pray for me to Our Lord that, instead of merely writing something, I may *be* something, and indeed that I may so fully be what I ought to be that there may be no further necessity for me to write, since the mere fact of being what I ought to be would be more eloquent than many books.

A Prayer to Louis Massignon

Let us be united in our prayers. This I say not as a formula, but in desperate poverty and need, with everyone else who is in need, who is in exile, a captive like them who hungers for truth and cannot find truth. Let us pray together and mourn in our hearts, crying out to God, the God of Abraham, the God also of Agar and Ishmael. May He give you strength in your sufferings and may His angels stand over you at all times. May the Holy Mother of God console you. May the Savior of the world bless you.

A Prayer to the Sisters of Loretto Taking Final Vows

Wherever you may go from here, remember me and pray for me. I will also remember you and keep you in my prayers. Since our Lord has made us neighbors and friends on earth, I presume He wants us to be neighbors and friends in heaven, too. But first we must accomplish our assigned tasks on this earth, whatever they may be. Let us keep praying for one another that we may do this well, with confidence and with joy, without anxiety, trusting in Him to whom we all belong.

A Prayer to Mary Luke Tobin

Pray for me to be a real good hermit and listen to the word of God and respond like a man. That is what it really involves: simply to stand on one's feet before one's Father and reply to Him in the Spirit.

This business about replying to the Father in the Spirit may sound like big talk but I don't mean it that way. "In the Spirit," in any context I know of, means flat on your face.

How one can stand on one's own feet and be flat on one's face at the same time is a mystery I will have to try to work out by living it.

A Prayer to Jailed Ladies

Keep me in your pocket if you have one.

Keep me in your heart if you have no pocket.

A Litany to Everybody

All holy souls,
pray for us fellows,
all Carmelites pray,
all Third Orders,
all sodalities
all altar societies
all action groups,
all inaction groups
all beat up shut in groups
all without money groups,
pray for the rich Trappist cheese groups
vice versa
mutual help,
amen, amen.

A Prayer of Thanksgiving
Written for Victor Hammer

O Tu, Pater Splendoris Dator luminis
Ad Te gaudens precor restituto lumine
Da quaesumus mihi servulo tecum perpetuam
Nox ubi non contristet corda vel umbra diem.

O Thou Father of Splendor, Giver of Light,
To Thee I pray in joy, with light restored.
Grant, I beg, to me Thy servant everlasting
Day in which no night makes sad the heart
And no shadow the day.

A Prayer for Peace

(From a prayer read in the House of Representatives
on April 12, 1962, Wednesday in Holy Week)

Almighty and merciful God, Father of all, Creator and Ruler of
the Universe, Lord of History Whose designs are inscrutable,
Whose glory is without blemish, Whose compassion for our
errors is inexhaustible,

in Your will is our peace.

Mercifully hear this prayer which rises to You from the tumult
and desperation of a world in which You are forgotten, in which
Your name is not invoked, Your laws are derided, Your presence
is ignored.

Because we do not know You, we have no peace.

Help us to be masters of the weapons that threaten to master
us. Help us to use our science for peace and plenty, not for war
and destruction. Show us how to use nuclear power to bless
our children's children, not to blight them.

Resolve our inner contradictions that now grow beyond belief
and beyond bearing. They are at once a torment and a blessing:
for if You had not left us the light of conscience, we would not
have to endure them. Teach us to be long-suffering in anguish
and insecurity. Teach us to wait and trust. Grant light, grant
strength and patience to all who work for peace.

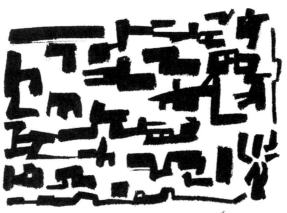

tM. '60.

Grant us Prudence in proportion to our power, Wisdom in proportion to our science and Humaneness in proportion to our wealth and might. Bless our earnest will to help all races and people to travel in friendship along the road to justice, liberty and lasting peace.

Grant us above all to see that our ways are not necessarily Your ways, that we cannot fully penetrate the mystery of Your designs and that the very storm of power now raging on this earth reveals Your hidden will and Your inscrutable decision. Grant us to see Your face in the lightning of this cosmic storm, O God of holiness, merciful to all. Grant us to seek peace where it is truly found!

In Your will, O God, is our peace! Amen.

A Prayer in Asia

O God, we are one with You. You have made us one with You. You have taught us that, if we are open to one another, You dwell in us. Help us to preserve this openness and to fight for it with all our hearts. Help us to realize that there can be no understanding where there is mutual rejection.

O God, in accepting one another wholeheartedly, fully, completely, we accept You, and we thank You, and we adore You, and we love You with our being, because our being is in Your being, our spirit is rooted in Your Spirit.

Fill us then with love and let us be bound together with love as we go our diverse ways, united in this one Spirit which makes You present to the world, and which makes You witness to the ultimate reality that is love.

Love has overcome. Love is victorious. Amen.

Word, the whole universe swells with Thy wide-open
    speech,
Father, the whole world bursts, breaks, huge Spirit, with
    Thy might
Then land, sea and wind swing
And roll from my forgotten feet
While God sings victory, sings victory
In the blind day of that defeat.

O little forests, meekly
Touch the snow with low branches!
O covered stones
Hide the house of growth!

Secret
Vegetal words,
Unlettered water,
Daily zero.

Pray undistracted
Curled tree
Carved in steel!—
Buried zenith!

Fire, turn inward
To your weak fort,
To a burly infant spot,
A house of nothing.

O peace, bless this mad place:
Silence, love this growth.

O silence, golden zero
Unsetting sun

Love winter when the plant says nothing.

Sources and Notes

SOURCES:
PUBLICATION INFORMATION FOR MERTON TITLES
Merton references are cited here in full. The notes that follow refer to these references by title only.

A Search for Solitude, edited by Lawrence S. Cunningham. San Francisco: HarperSanFrancisco, 1997.

The Asian Journal of Thomas Merton, edited by James Laughlin, Naomi Burton Stone, and Patrick Hart. New York: New Directions Press, 1973.

The Climate of Monastic Prayer. Washington, D.C.: Cistercian Publications, 1973.

The Collected Poems of Thomas Merton. New York: New Directions Press, 1977.

Day of a Stranger. Salt Lake City: Smith, 1981.

Draft of *The Seven Storey Mountain*. Unpublished manuscript in the Thomas Merton Collection. New York: Columbia University Library.

Entering the Silence, edited by Jonathan Montaldo. San Francisco: HarperSanFrancisco, 1997.

The Hidden Ground of Love, edited by William H. Shannon. New York: Farrar, Straus & Giroux, 1985.

Learning to Love, edited by Christine M. Bochen. San Francisco: HarperSanFrancisco, 1998.

"Meditations, December, 1941." Unpublished manuscript in the Mark Van Doren Collection. New York: Columbia University Library.

No Man Is an Island. New York: Harcourt, Brace & Company, 1955.

The Nonviolent Alternative, edited by Gordon C. Zahn. New York: Farrar, Straus & Giroux, 1980.

The Road to Joy, edited by Robert E. Daggy. New York: Farrar, Straus & Giroux, 1989.

Run to the Mountain, edited by Patrick Hart. San Francisco: HarperSanFrancisco, 1996.

The School of Charity, edited by Patrick Hart. New York: Farrar, Straus & Giroux, 1990.

The Seven Storey Mountain. New York: Harcourt, Brace & Company, 1948.

The Sign of Jonas. New York: Harcourt, Brace & Company, 1953.

Thoughts in Solitude. New York: Farrar, Straus & Cudahy, 1958.

Turning Toward the World, edited by Victor A. Kramer. San Francisco: HarperSanFrancisco, 1997.

Witness to Freedom, edited by William H. Shannon. New York: Farrar, Straus & Giroux, 1994.

NOTES

Epigraph page ix. *Thoughts in Solitude*, 83.

Introduction

"The only unhappiness . . . ," *Entering the Silence*, 64.

"Marvelous vision . . . ," *Turning Toward the World*, 321–22.

"The true contemplative . . . ," *The Climate of Monastic Prayer*, 122–23.

"Your brightness . . . ," "Meditations, December, 1941," 2.

"To return to the Father . . . ," *Turning Toward the World*, 101.

"I have a simple way . . . ," *The Hidden Ground of Love*, 63–64.

Prayers

1. *Thoughts in Solitude*, 101.

1. *A Search for Solitude*, 16.

1. *Day of a Stranger*, 41.

3. "The Reader," *The Collected Poems of Thomas Merton*, 202.

5. *Run to the Mountain*, 310; "Meditations, December, 1941," 2.

7. "SACRED HEART 2," *The Collected Poems of Thomas Merton*, 24.

9. *Run to the Mountain*, 399.

11. *Run to the Mountain*, 470–71.

13. *The Seven Storey Mountain*, 419.

15. *The Seven Storey Mountain*, 419–20.

17. Draft of *The Seven Storey Mountain*, 686.

19. *The Seven Storey Mountain*, 421.

21. *The Seven Storey Mountain*, 421–22.

23. *Entering the Silence*, 46.

25. *Entering the Silence*, 5.

27. *Entering the Silence*, 49.

29. *Entering the Silence*, 49.

31. *Entering the Silence*, 67–68.

33. *Entering the Silence*, 70.

35. *Entering the Silence*, 71.

37. "Evening: Zero Weather," *The Collected Poems of Thomas Merton*, 174.

39. *Entering the Silence*, 77–78.

41. *Entering the Silence*, 87.

43. *Entering the Silence*, 101–2.

45. *Entering the Silence*, 101.

47. *Entering the Silence*, 127.

49. *Entering the Silence*, 127.

51. *Entering the Silence*, 134; *The Sign of Jonas*, 76.

53. *The Sign of Jonas*, 76.

55. *Entering the Silence*, 177.

57. *Entering the Silence*, 161.

59. *Entering the Silence*, 178–79.

61. *Entering the Silence*, 202.

63. *Entering the Silence*, 376.

65. *Entering the Silence*, 404.

67. *Entering the Silence*, 417–18.

69. *Entering the Silence*, 473.

71. *Run to the Mountain*, 400.

73. *Entering the Silence*, 477.

75. *Entering the Silence*, 480–81.

77. *Entering the Silence*, 481.

79. *Entering the Silence*, 482–83.

81. *Entering the Silence*, 483.

83. *Entering the Silence*, 483.

85. *Entering the Silence*, 487.

87. *Entering the Silence*, 487.

89. *Entering the Silence*, 487.

91. *Entering the Silence*, 487.

93. *Entering the Silence*, 487–88.

95. *Entering the Silence*, 488.

97. *A Search for Solitude*, 14–15.

99. *A Search for Solitude*, 30.

101. *The Sign of Jonas*, 334.

103. *A Search for Solitude*, 61–62.

105. *A Search for Solitude*, 63.

107. *No Man Is an Island*, 232.

109. *Thoughts in Solitude*, 38–39.

111. *Thoughts in Solitude*, 71–72.

113. *Thoughts in Solitude*, 72.

115. *Thoughts in Solitude*, 99–100.

117. *Thoughts in Solitude*, 121–22.

119. *Thoughts in Solitude*, 122–23.

121. *Turning Toward the World*, 28.

123. *Turning Toward the World*, 120.

125. *Turning Toward the World*, 120–21.

127. "The Biography," *The Collected Poems of Thomas Merton*, 104.

129. "To the Immaculate Virgin, On a Winter Night," *The Collected Poems of Thomas Merton*, 219.

131. *The Seven Storey Mountain*, 129–30.

133. *The Seven Storey Mountain*, 282.

135. *Entering the Silence*, 32.

137. *Entering the Silence*, 112, 123.

139. *A Search for Solitude*, 46.

141. *A Search for Solitude*, 46–47.

143. *Entering the Silence*, 105–6.

145. *Entering the Silence*, 385.

147. *Entering the Silence*, 386.

149. *Entering the Silence*, 253.

151. *Learning to Love*, 360.

153. *A Search for Solitude*, 277.

155. *The Seven Storey Mountain*, 130.

157. *The Road to Joy*, 153.

159. *The Hidden Ground of Love*, 137.

161. *The School of Charity*, 31.

163. *Witness to Freedom*, 280.

165. *Witness to Freedom,* 54.

167. *The School of Charity,* 288–89.

169. "There Has to Be a Jail for Ladies," *The Collected Poems of Thomas Merton,* 332.

171. "Litany," *The Collected Poems of Thomas Merton,* 724–25.

173. *Witness to Freedom,* 10.

175. *The Non-Violent Alternative,* 268–69.

177. *The Non-Violent Alternative,* 269–70.

179. *The Asian Journal of Thomas Merton,* 318–19.

181. "Hymn for the Feast of Duns Scotus," *The Collected Poems of Thomas Merton,* 199.

183. "Love Winter When the Plant Says Nothing," *The Collected Poems of Thomas Merton,* 353.